UnBoxed
UncoveringNewParadigms

STUDY GUIDE

Martijn van Tilborgh

Copyright © 2020 by Martijn van Tilborgh

Published by Avail Publishing

All rights reserved. No portion of this book may be reproduced, stored in a retrieval system, or transmitted in any form or by any means—electronic, mechanical, photocopy, recording, scanning, or other—except for brief quotations in critical reviews or articles, without prior written permission of the author.

Scripture quotations marked KJV are taken from the King James Version of the Bible. Public domain. Scripture quotations marked NIV are taken from the Holy Bible, New International Version®, NIV®. Copyright © 1973, 1978, 1984, 2011 by Biblica, Inc.™ Used by permission of Zondervan. All rights reserved worldwide. www.zondervan.com. The "NIV" and "New International Version" are trademarks registered in the United States Patent and Trademark Office by Biblica, Inc.™ | Scripture quotations marked NKJV are taken from the New King James Version®. Copyright © 1982 by Thomas Nelson. Used by permission. All rights reserved. | Scripture quotations marked TLB are taken from The Living Bible copy- right © 1971 by Tyndale House Foundation. Used by permission of Tyndale House Publishers Inc., Carol Stream, Illinois 60188. All rights reserved. The Living Bible, TLB, and The Living Bible logo are registered trademarks of Tyndale House Publishers. | Scripture quotations marked NLT are taken from the *Holy Bible*, New Living Translation, copyright © 1996, 2004, 2015 by Tyndale House Foundation. Used by permission of Tyndale House Publishers, Inc., Carol Stream, Illinois 60188. All rights reserved. | Scripture quotations marked MSG are taken from *THE MESSAGE*, copyright © 1993, 1994, 1995, 1996, 2000, 2001, 2002 by Eugene H. Peterson. Used by permission of NavPress. All rights reserved. Represented by Tyndale House Publishers, Inc. | Scripture quotations marked GNT are from the Good News Translation in Today's English Version—Second Edition. Copyright © 1992 by American Bible Society. Used by Permission.

For foreign and subsidiary rights, contact the author.

Interior Photos: © Shutterstock, Andrew van Tilborgh, Jessica Hegland, Dominic Fondon

ISBN: 978-1-950718-51-1   1 2 3 4 5 6 7 8 9 10

Printed in the United States of America

UnBoxed
UncoveringNewParadigms

STUDY GUIDE

Martijn van Tilborgh

CONTENTS

6   INTRODUCTION

12   CHAPTER 1
The Advantage Factor

18   CHAPTER 2
Someone Is Waiting for You

24   CHAPTER 3
A Mexican Blanket
and a Cheap Bottle of Booze

30   CHAPTER 4
How to Become the Best Mediocre You

36   CHAPTER 5
Getting Unboxed: Step by Step

42   CHAPTER 6
Think Bigger

48   CHAPTER 7
Get Out

54   CHAPTER 8
Destroy the Box

60   CHAPTER 9
Create

66   CHAPTER 10
Boxes Kill Dreams

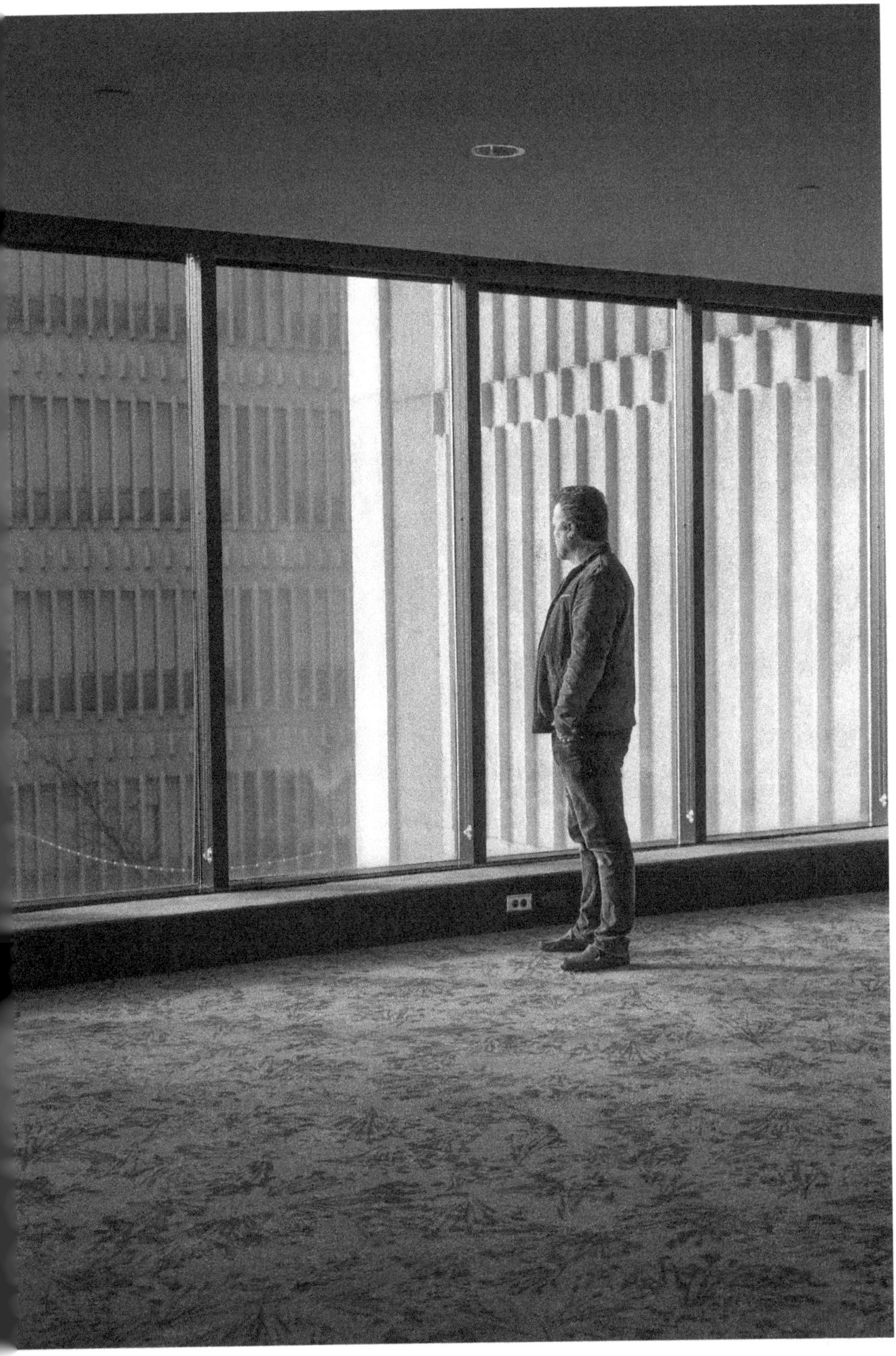

Introduction

○ ○ ○

"I didn't realize, really, that I had put myself in a box. And it was a box that looked so big from the inside. But from God's viewpoint, it was too small. In context of what I am able to see today, I realize how insignificant that box really was—in light of what God had, and still has, in store for me. I needed some sort of intervention to show me a bigger world. I needed to be unboxed!"

READ / Introduction

READING TIME

Read the Introduction to *Unboxed*. Use the Notes space to record any thoughts you want to remember or questions you want to talk about later.

OPENING THOUGHTS /

Why do you think it's so important to remove the boxes, or ways of thinking, that limit us in our leadership?

_____
_____
_____
_____
_____
_____

Think about one thing you're looking to learn about from this study, or one area in which you want to improve. What is it? Why is this important to your leadership growth and development?

_____
_____
_____
_____
_____
_____

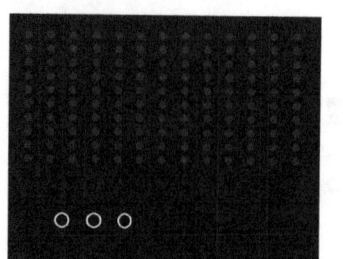

STUDY SCRIPTURE

Read Matthew 13:45-46: "Again, the kingdom of heaven is like a merchant seeking beautiful pearls, who, when he had found one pearl of great price, went and sold all that he had and bought it."

○ ○ ○

What differences are there between what the merchant was seeking and what he ultimately found?

_____
_____
_____
_____
_____
_____

How do we see the merchant's true commitment to the pearl displayed? How will others see your commitment to your purpose?

_____
_____
_____
_____
_____
_____

RESPOND /

What part of Martijn's journey most inspires you or stokes your curiosity?

_____
_____
_____
_____
_____

SHARE YOUR STORY

"When God speaks, a single word from His mouth can change everything!"

○ ○ ○

How have you come to see with a broader perspective in the past? What do you think some of the contributing factors have been that caused you to see a bigger world?

_____
_____
_____
_____
_____
_____

Why do you think we so easily settle for what we currently enjoy, instead of looking ahead for more?

_____
_____
_____
_____
_____

What paradigms or ways of thinking are holding you back? How have they limited your leadership capacity?

_____
_____
_____
_____
_____

Unboxed: Study Guide | 9

○ ○ ○

Choose one of those boxes. What's one step you can take today to begin stepping outside of that box?

_____
_____
_____
_____

What about your team? What boxes are holding them back?

_____
_____
_____
_____

How can you begin to dismantle those boxes, leading your team in an unboxing process that starts with yourself?

_____
_____
_____
_____

Unboxed: Study Guide | 11

CHAPTER 1

The Advantage Factor

○ ○ ○

"It's funny how our human minds work. We always tend to default back to what we know, based on our past experiences or the way we were raised or the things we were taught and the culture we grew up in."

READ / Chapter 1

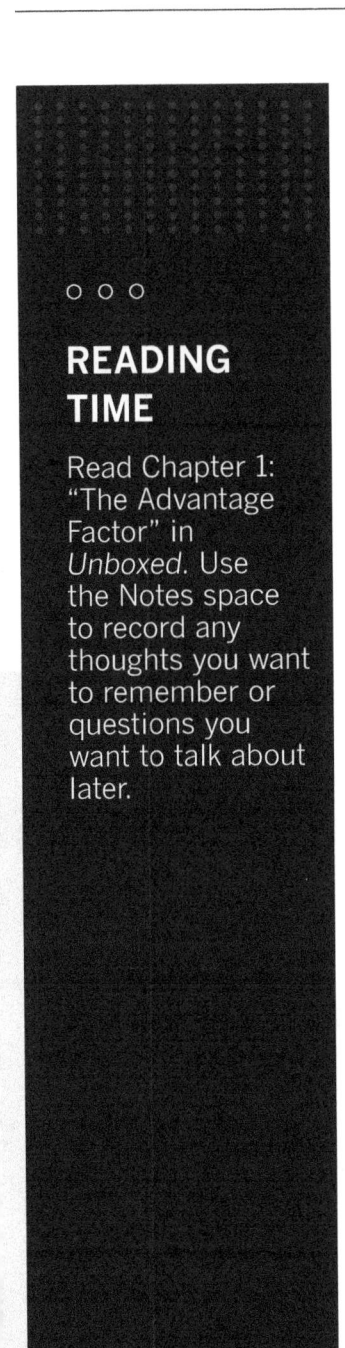

READING TIME

Read Chapter 1: "The Advantage Factor" in *Unboxed*. Use the Notes space to record any thoughts you want to remember or questions you want to talk about later.

OPENING THOUGHTS /

Why do you think it's so important to remove the boxes, or ways of thinking, that limit us in our leadership?

_____
_____
_____
_____
_____

Think about one thing you're looking to learn about from this study, or one area in which you want to improve. What is it? Why is this important to your leadership growth and development?

_____
_____
_____
_____
_____
_____

SHARE YOUR STORY

"I realized I was experiencing the things I was going through because of an advantage the Lord wanted to show me outside of the box I was in."

○ ○ ○

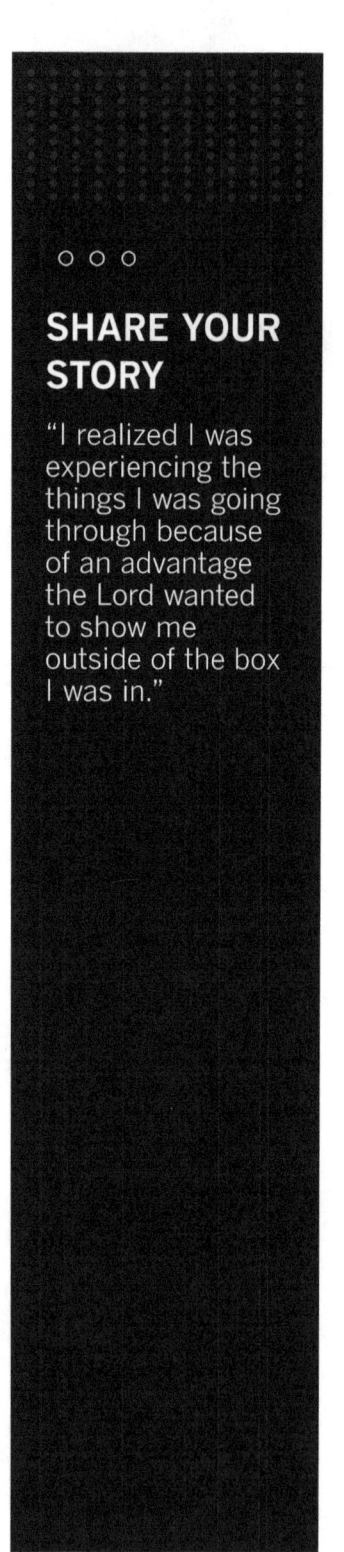

What might God be trying to show you in those areas? What better things might He have for you?

_____
_____
_____
_____
_____

Have you ever kept or stayed near some part of your leadership that was "dead"? What made you want to stay?

_____
_____
_____
_____
_____

What made you finally walk away from that dead thing?

_____
_____
_____
_____
_____

STUDY SCRIPTURE

Read John 16:5-7: "But now I go away to Him who sent Me, and none of you asks Me, 'Where are You going?' But because I have said these things to you, sorrow has filled your heart. Nevertheless I tell you the truth. It is to your advantage that I go away; for if I do not go away, the Helper will not come to you; but if I depart, I will send Him to you."

○ ○ ○

How do you think Jesus's followers felt when He told them their current way of life— living, eating, traveling, and ministering with Jesus— had to stop?

_____
_____
_____
_____
_____
_____

Have you ever had to let go of something as a leader that, in the long run, actually benefitted you and those you serve? How did you come to realize this?

_____
_____
_____
_____
_____

What areas of frustration or confusion exist right now in your life? In what areas are you asking, "Now what?"

_____
_____
_____
_____
_____
_____
_____

○ ○ ○

Why do you think we hang onto a false sense of productivity or accomplishment, especially as leaders? What precedent does this set for those who serve underneath us?

_____
_____
_____
_____

How does your perspective need to change in order for you to let go of what you no longer need right now?

_____
_____
_____
_____

What specific steps do you need to take to let go of the "dead" things in your life?

_____
_____
_____
_____

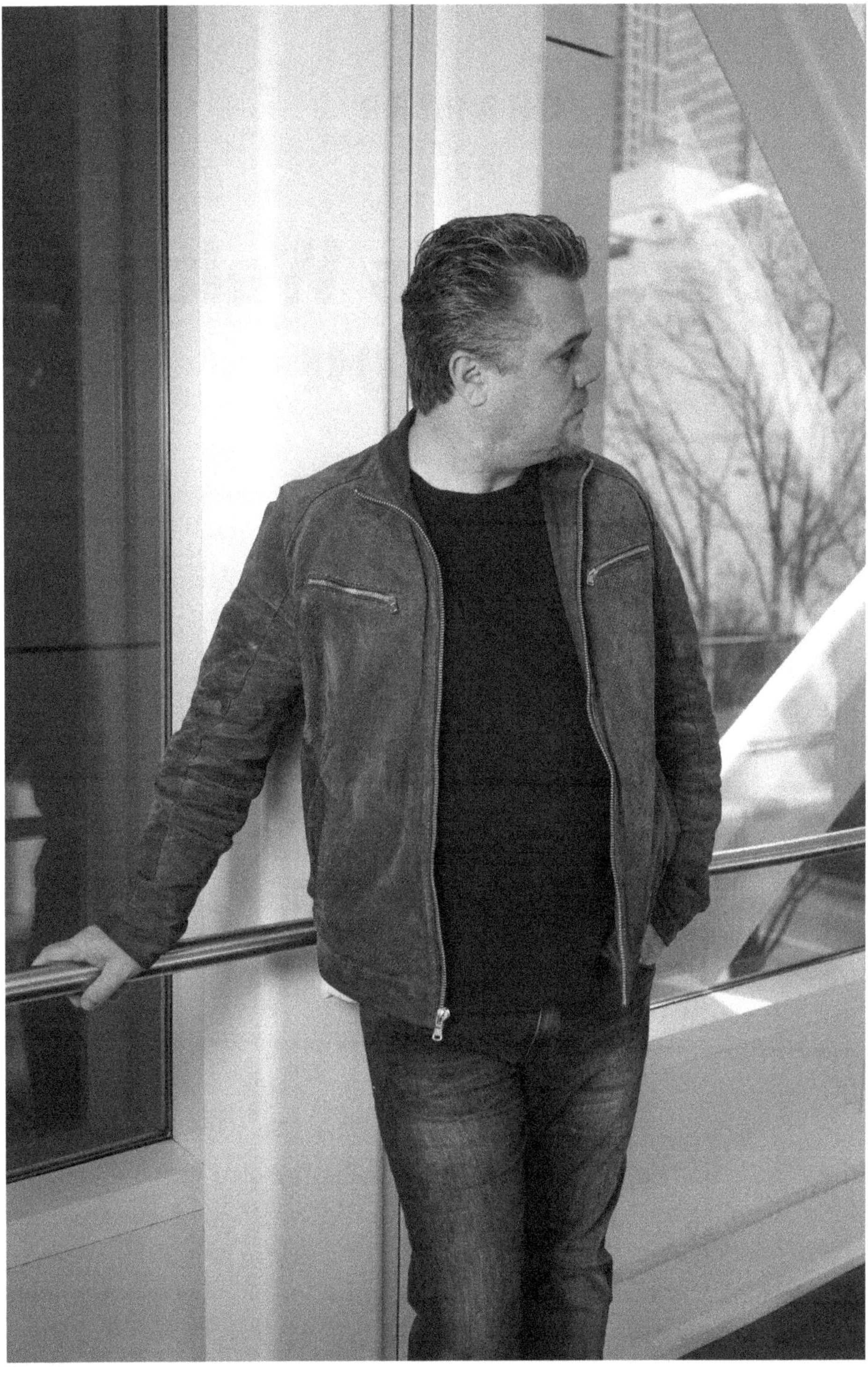

CHAPTER 2

Someone Is Waiting for You

○ ○ ○

"Creation is waiting for the sons of God to be revealed in the earth. The world around us is waiting for you and me to become who we are supposed to be. Creation waits for a full manifestation of God in and through you so that His kingdom can become visible on earth the same way it is already manifest in heaven."

READ / Chapter 2

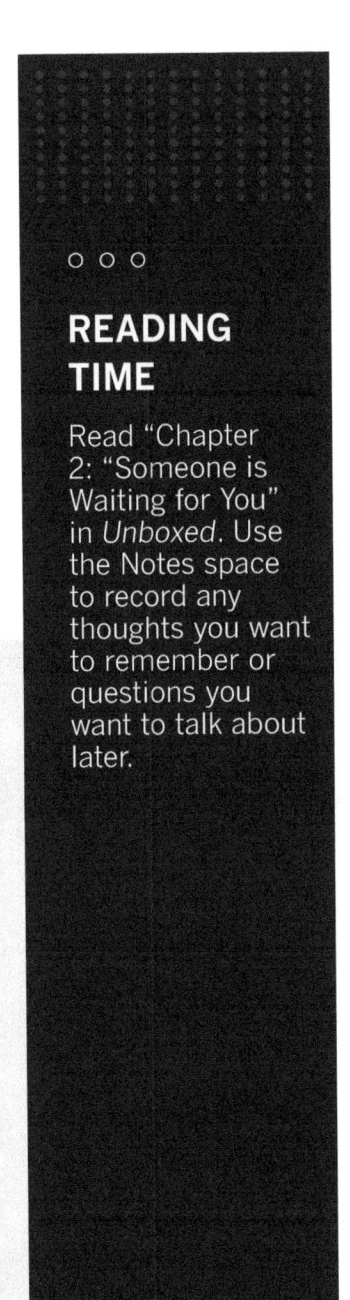

READING TIME

Read "Chapter 2: "Someone is Waiting for You" in *Unboxed*. Use the Notes space to record any thoughts you want to remember or questions you want to talk about later.

OPENING THOUGHTS /

Why do you think it's so difficult for us to move beyond our status quo, and reach for more in leadership and in life?

_____
_____
_____
_____
_____
_____

Who might stand to benefit from you when you step out of the box and pursue a more abundant life?

_____
_____
_____
_____
_____
_____

○ ○ ○

STUDY SCRIPTURE

Read John 10:7-10: "Most assuredly, I say to you, I am the door of the sheep. All who ever came before Me are thieves and robbers, but the sheep did not hear them. I am the door. If anyone enters by Me, he will be saved, and will go in and out and find pasture. The thief does not come except to steal, and to kill, and to destroy. I have come that they may have life, and that they may have it more abundantly."

○ ○ ○

How can the abundance we are meant to experience benefit others around us, as well?

_____
_____
_____
_____
_____

What differences do you see between society's idea of "abundance" and what this Scripture is describing?

_____
_____
_____
_____
_____

Why do you think that, at times, our opposition comes disguised as something beneficial instead of being overt and obvious?

_____
_____
_____
_____
_____

SHARE YOUR STORY

"Many times, [the enemy] comes camouflaged as an angel of light. He even takes on a religious appearance in an attempt to keep us from greatness, while using the Word of God against us— to his advantage."

○ ○ ○

Have you ever believed you were living the abundant life, only to realize that there was more?

_____
_____
_____
_____
_____
_____

What brought you to this realization?

_____
_____
_____
_____
_____

What negative effects has "the thief" had in your leadership or personal life?

_____
_____
_____
_____
_____

○ ○ ○

What negative effects has "the thief" had in the lives of those you serve with and lead?

_____
_____
_____
_____

How does our culture, or society's values, contribute to the urge to chase comfort, status quo, and stagnation?

_____
_____
_____
_____

In what areas of your leadership have you currently settled for the status quo, even when you know there is more abundant life to be had?

_____
_____
_____
_____

Who are some of the leaders who inspire you— leaders who haven't settled, but have hungered for more and pursued it?

_____
_____
_____
_____

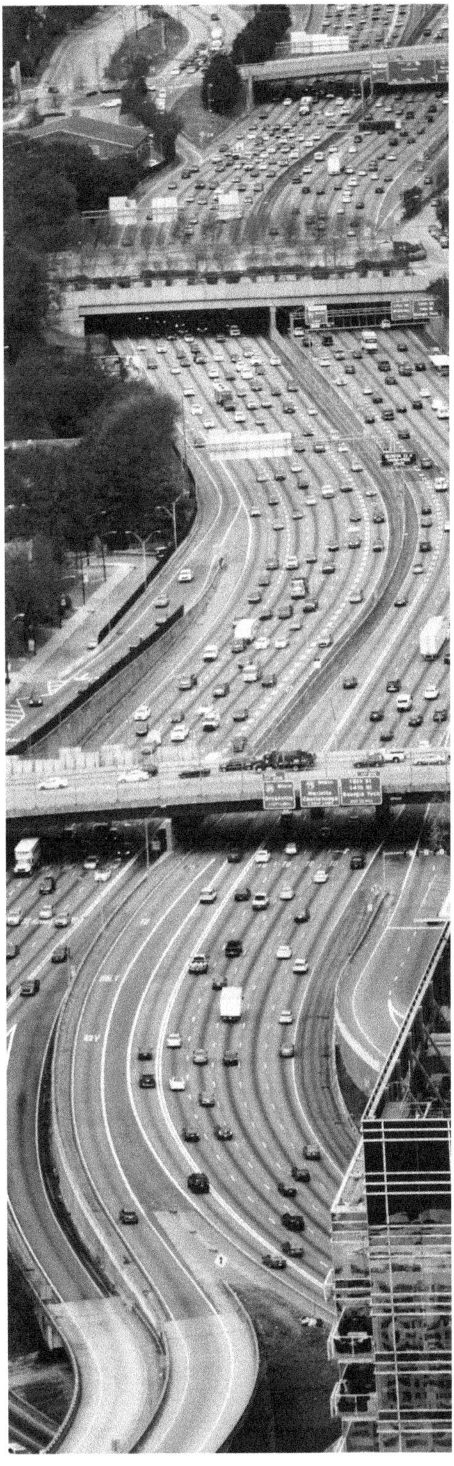

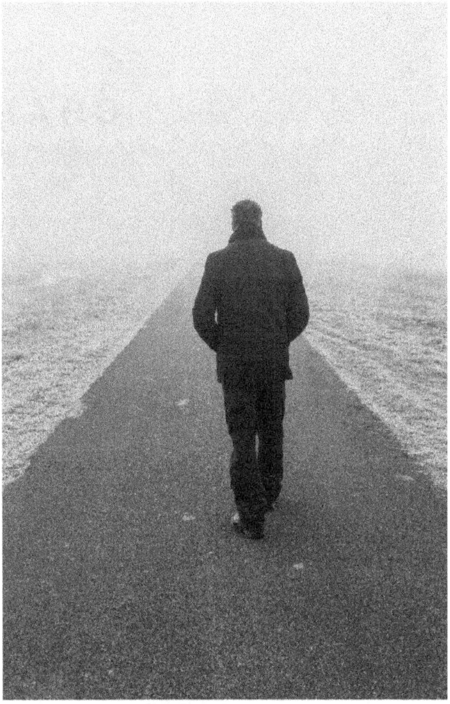

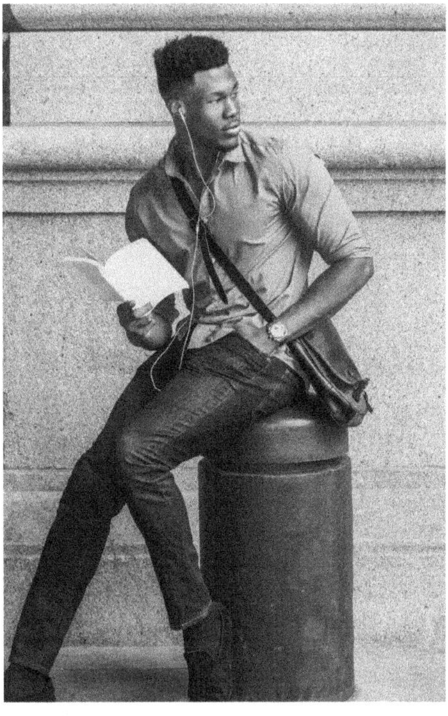

CHAPTER 3

A Mexican Blanket and a Cheap Bottle of Booze

○ ○ ○

"We do the things we do because we've been taught those things from a young age. Our behavior is rooted in how we've been raised; the culture in which we were brought up contributed to behavioral patterns. In turn, those patterns led us to create limitations and boxes for ourselves over the years."

READ / Chapter 3

READING TIME

Read Chapter 3: "A Mexican Blanket and a Bottle of Cheap Booze' in *Unboxed*. Use the Notes space to record any thoughts you want to remember or questions you want to talk about later.

OPENING THOUGHTS /

What "boxes" have you created for yourself based upon your upbringing or culture?

_____
_____
_____
_____
_____
_____

Why do you think it's so uncomfortable to embrace change, even when it's healthy?

_____
_____
_____
_____
_____
_____

○ ○ ○

STUDY SCRIPTURE

Read Romans 12:1-2: "I beseech you therefore, brethren, by the mercies of God, that you present your bodies a living sacrifice, holy, acceptable to God, which is your reasonable service. And do not be conformed to this world, but be transformed by the renewing of your mind, that you may prove what is that good and acceptable and perfect will of God."

○ ○ ○

In your own words, what's the difference between being conformed to the world's ways of doing things, and capitalizing on a good strategy that others happened to create?

___

In what areas are you moved to separate from the methods and perspectives of the world, in favor of a new, transformative paradigm?

___

Have you ever seen a paradigm, or a certain way of thinking, actually create problems that weren't there before?

___

SHARE YOUR STORY

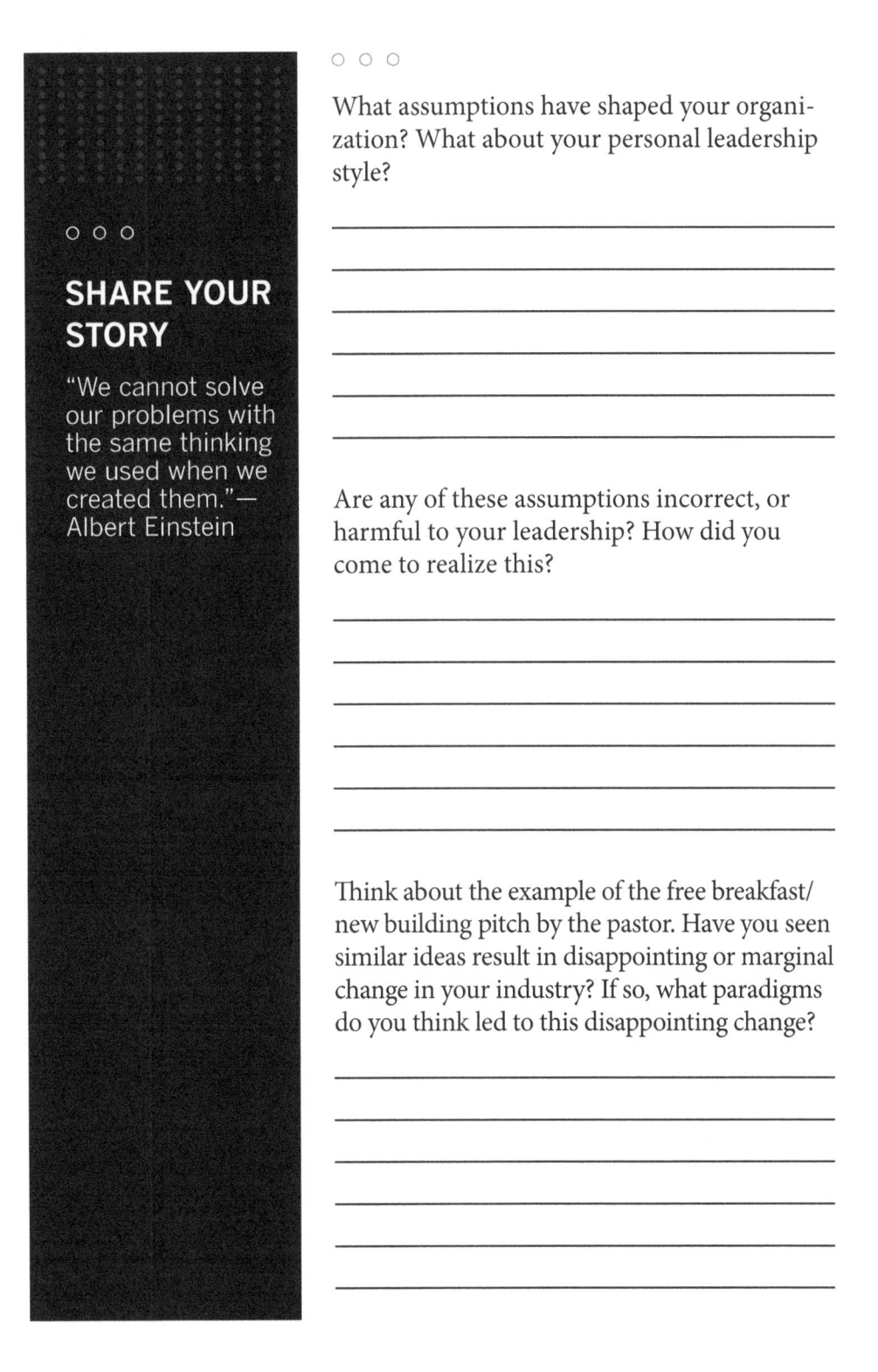

"We cannot solve our problems with the same thinking we used when we created them." — Albert Einstein

○ ○ ○

What assumptions have shaped your organization? What about your personal leadership style?

_____
_____
_____
_____
_____
_____

Are any of these assumptions incorrect, or harmful to your leadership? How did you come to realize this?

_____
_____
_____
_____
_____

Think about the example of the free breakfast/new building pitch by the pastor. Have you seen similar ideas result in disappointing or marginal change in your industry? If so, what paradigms do you think led to this disappointing change?

_____
_____
_____
_____
_____
_____

○ ○ ○

Why do you think it's easier to operate by the same paradigms everyone else is using?

_____
_____
_____
_____

What potential benefit do we stand to gain by breaking out of these boxes and operating based on new paradigms?

_____
_____
_____
_____

After reading this chapter, what's one thing you can begin to take action on in a fresh way, with a new perspective? What specific actions do you want to begin to take?

_____
_____
_____
_____

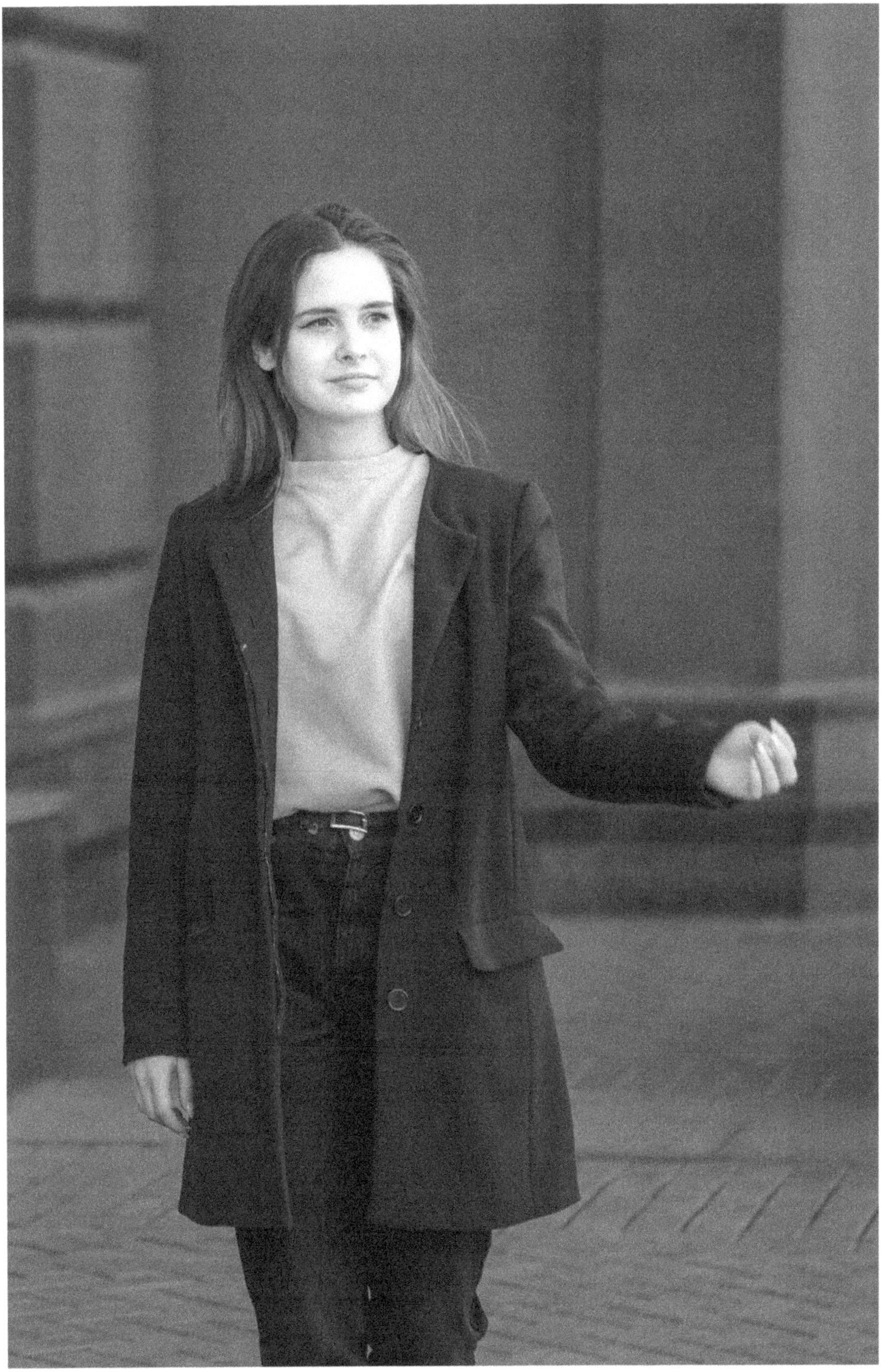

CHAPTER 4

How to Become the Best Mediocre You

"'Competition' is not a word that appears in God's dictionary. It is something that never was part of His original design for creation. Competition is something we created. Not as much because we invented it as much as our tendency to create religious boxes resulted in an environment in which competition lives."

READ / Chapter 4

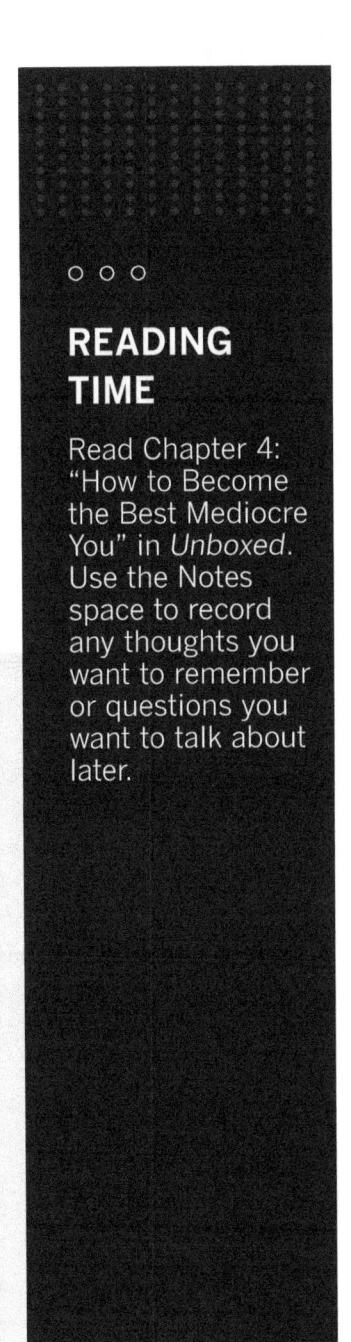

READING TIME

Read Chapter 4: "How to Become the Best Mediocre You" in *Unboxed*. Use the Notes space to record any thoughts you want to remember or questions you want to talk about later.

OPENING THOUGHTS /

Why do you think we tend to compare and compete with others?

In what areas do you find yourself currently competing with others, whether or not they know you're doing so?

○ ○ ○

STUDY SCRIPTURE

Read Luke 7:26-28: "But what did you go out to see? A prophet? Yes, I say to you, and more than a prophet. This is he of whom it is written:'Behold, I send My messenger before Your face, Who will prepare Your way before You.' For I say to you, among those born of women there is not a greater prophet than John the Baptist; but he who is least in the kingdom of God is greater than he."

○ ○ ○

What's the potential appeal of a world in which, if you just try hard enough, you can be #1, above everybody else?

_____
_____
_____
_____
_____
_____

How is the competitive paradigm actually much more harmful than it seems?

_____
_____
_____
_____
_____
_____

Do you think the majority of leaders are satisfied with becoming the best mediocre versions of themselves? Why or why not?

_____
_____
_____
_____
_____
_____

SHARE YOUR STORY

"We focus on how we can earn more points on the scoreboard, not realizing the scoreboard we're looking at is referencing how we rank in a world of mediocrity. The best thing that can happen to us within that "system" is that you and I become the best mediocre versions of ourselves that we can be."

○ ○ ○

How can you go about creating a new category to be Number 1 in? What specific talents and proficiencies do you bring to the table that help inform that new category?

_____
_____
_____
_____
_____
_____

What does it make you feel to know that there are an infinite number of categories— that you are created utterly uniquely?

_____
_____
_____
_____
_____
_____

Why is it essential to change our way of thinking—to become unboxed— before our ways of behavior change?

_____
_____
_____
_____
_____
_____

○ ○ ○

Think about 1-3 concrete steps you can take today to begin to differentiate what you offer from the rest of the field. How can you begin to move from competition to innovation?

_____
_____
_____
_____

How can you enlist the support and help of those you lead? What about mentors and coaches in your life?

_____
_____
_____
_____

You have unique skills and passions. How will becoming unboxed allow you to more fully pursue and perfect those gifts?

_____
_____
_____
_____

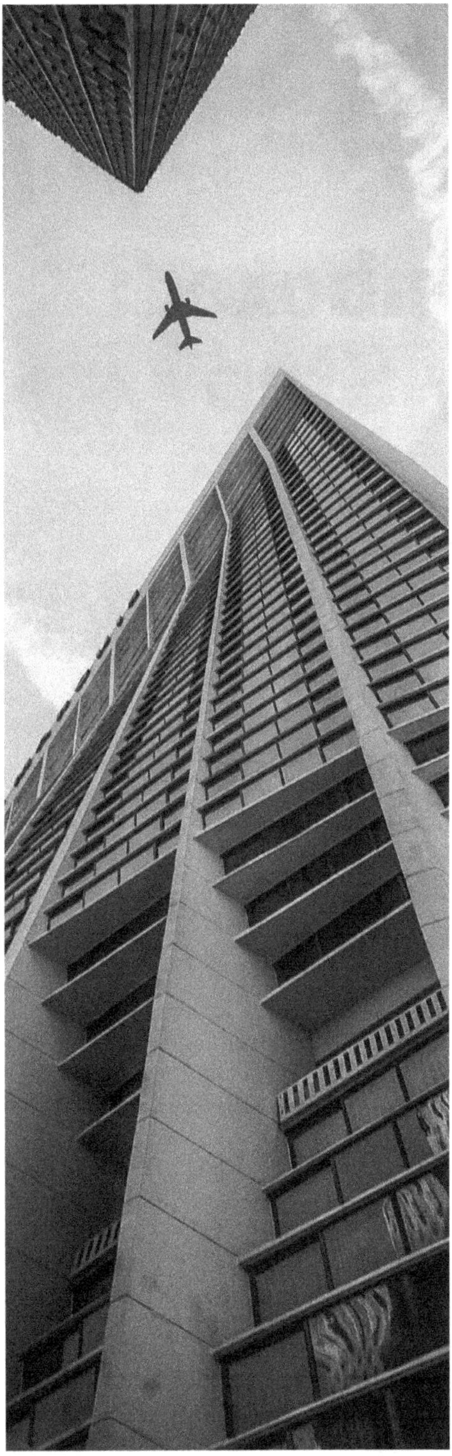

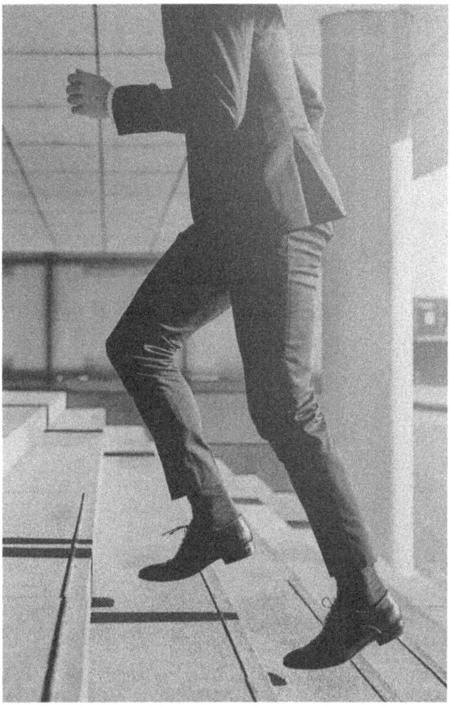

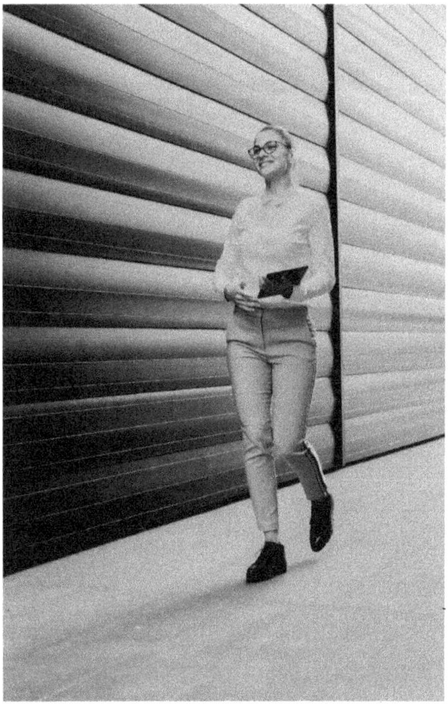

CHAPTER 5

Getting Unboxed: Step by Step

○ ○ ○

"So often we find ourselves in the same position as John. God has an open door for us, but we can't see beyond that door because of our vantage point. We somehow need to shift in order to be able to see beyond it. On the other side of the open door there are things that must take place. Things pertaining to our future."

READ / Introduction

READING TIME

Read Chapter 5: "Getting Unboxed: Step by Step" in *Unboxed*. Use the Notes space to record any thoughts you want to remember or questions you want to talk about later.

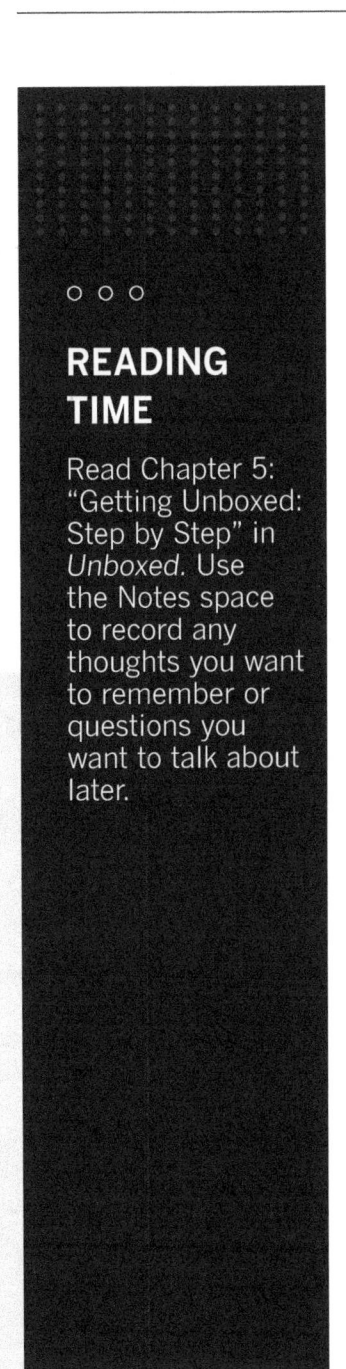

OPENING THOUGHTS /

How does our vantage point dictate how we go about leading and pursuing our purpose? How can a false perspective cause us to veer off-course?

_____
_____
_____
_____
_____
_____

The first step of the unboxing process is awareness. What's one area in your leadership in which you recognize a need for increased awareness?

_____
_____
_____
_____
_____
_____

○ ○ ○

STUDY SCRIPTURE

Read Zechariah 2:2-5: "Then I raised my eyes and looked, and behold, a man with a measuring line in his hand. So I said, 'Where are you going?' And he said to me, 'To measure Jerusalem, to see what is its width and what is its length.' And there was the angel who talked with me, going out; and another angel was coming out to meet him, who said to him, 'Run, speak to this young man, saying: "Jerusalem shall be inhabited as towns without walls, because of the multitude of men and livestock in it. For I," says the Lord, "will be a wall of fire all around her, and I will be the glory in her midst."'"

○ ○ ○

What about this exchange stands out to you?

_____
_____
_____
_____
_____
_____

How can our passion and zeal sometimes mislead us, especially when it comes to leading others?

_____
_____
_____
_____
_____

Are there any areas in which you've unconsciously operated in opposition to what God wanted to do? How did you discover this?

_____
_____
_____
_____
_____

○ ○ ○

SHARE YOUR STORY

"Could it be that we have measuring lines in our minds that reference a standard that was not meant to be a standard to begin with? Could it be that we are working on assumptions that we need to be made aware of? Could it be that God is trying to remove the measuring lines by which we measure our work?"

○ ○ ○

What measuring tools are you currently using to determine your success?

_____
_____
_____
_____
_____
_____

Are these tools man-made? How do you know?

_____
_____
_____
_____
_____

How might God want to re-shape or re-define the measuring tools you're using? What new metrics might He want to introduce?

_____
_____
_____
_____
_____
_____

○ ○ ○

What's one "box" you have become aware of over the course of this study?

_____
_____
_____
_____

How is the box you listed above taking away from your leadership effectiveness and potential?

_____
_____
_____
_____

What potential detriment could this box have on your future if it remains in your life?

_____
_____
_____
_____

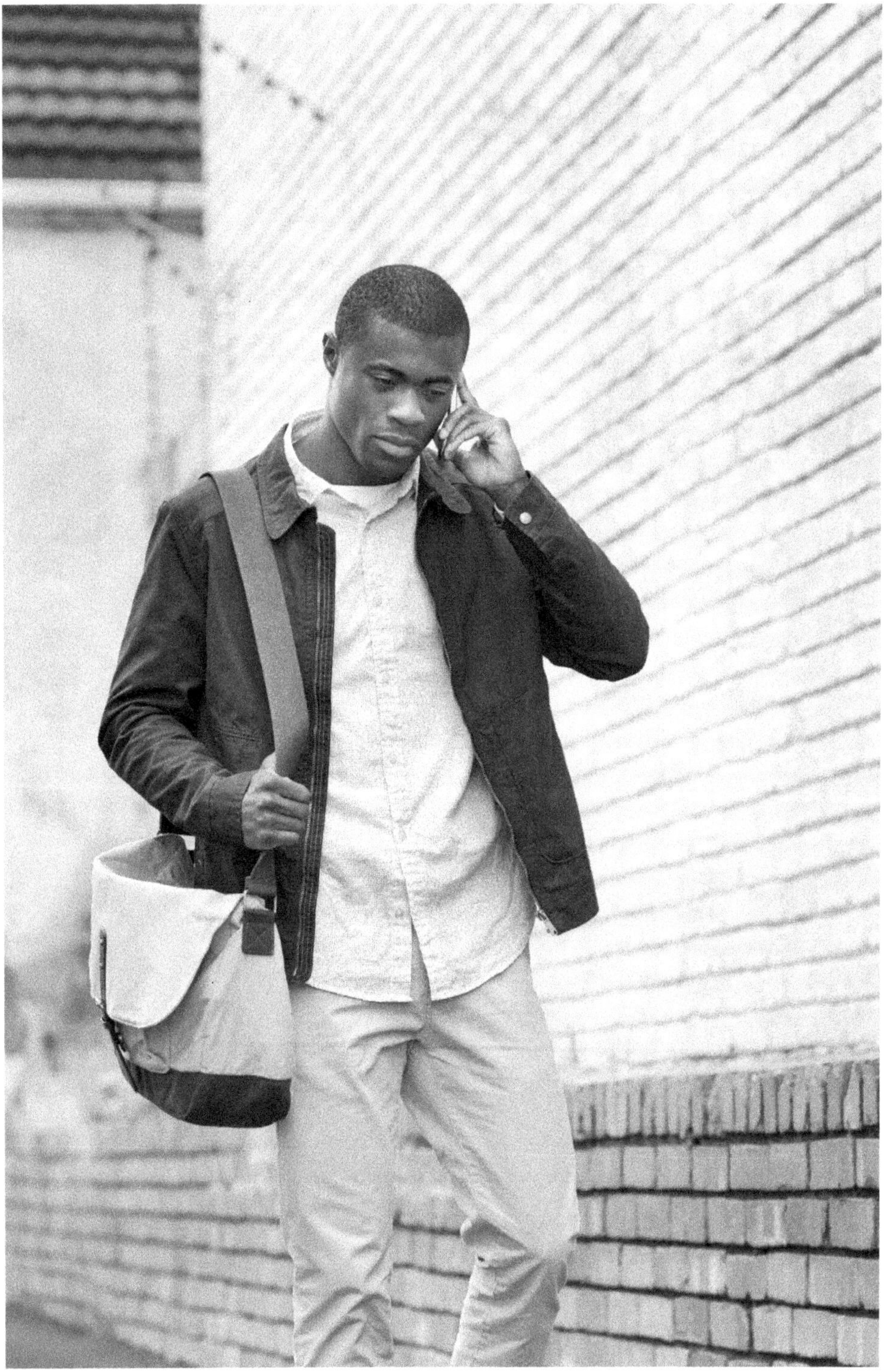

CHAPTER 6

Think Bigger

○ ○ ○

"Apparently it is possible for God's people to work their butts off and toil day and night to build something that is completely foreign to God's intended purpose. That's a scary thought, isn't it?"

READ / Introduction

READING TIME

Read Chapter 6: "Think Bigger" in *Unboxed*. Use the Notes space to record any thoughts you want to remember or questions you want to talk about later.

OPENING THOUGHTS /

Do you find it scary to consider the possibility that your beliefs could be wrong? Why or why not?

As a leader, why do you think it's important to become comfortable with being wrong and adjusting your views accordingly?

○ ○ ○

STUDY SCRIPTURE

Read Exodus 12:15. "Seven days you shall eat unleavened bread. On the first day you shall remove leaven from your houses. For whoever eats leavened bread from the first day until the seventh day, that person shall be cut off from Israel."

○ ○ ○

What was the main factor in the Israelites' remaining in bondage, according to this chapter?

_____
_____
_____
_____
_____
_____

How did the Israelites' misplaced efforts actually aid their enemy instead of their own purposes?

_____
_____
_____
_____
_____
_____

Why do you think it's so hard for us to let go of our preconceived ideas?

_____
_____
_____
_____
_____

SHARE YOUR STORY

"Making an inventory of your belief system is one of the best things you can do if you want to get out of your little box. In fact, it is a crucial step in getting out."

○ ○ ○

Are there any false beliefs you've had to let go of in the past as a leader? What brought you to a place where you were ready to release them?

_____
_____
_____
_____
_____
_____

Did you notice if any of those misplaced beliefs actually took away from your purpose, instead of advancing it? Did they cause you to inadvertently build "pyramids" with no life inside them?

_____
_____
_____
_____
_____
_____

The Israelites celebrated the feast of unleavened bread every year. How can a regular evaluation of our beliefs and doctrines help us avoid falling back into false beliefs?

_____
_____
_____
_____
_____

○ ○ ○

Have you sensed a cultural pressure to avoid thinking outside the box? If so, why do you think this pressure exists?

_____

_____

_____

_____

What power is there in being comfortable with being wrong once in a while?

_____

_____

_____

_____

Take some time to surrender all of the knowledge you have to the Lord, and ask Him to begin confirming or denying the truth of what you think you know.

_____

_____

_____

_____

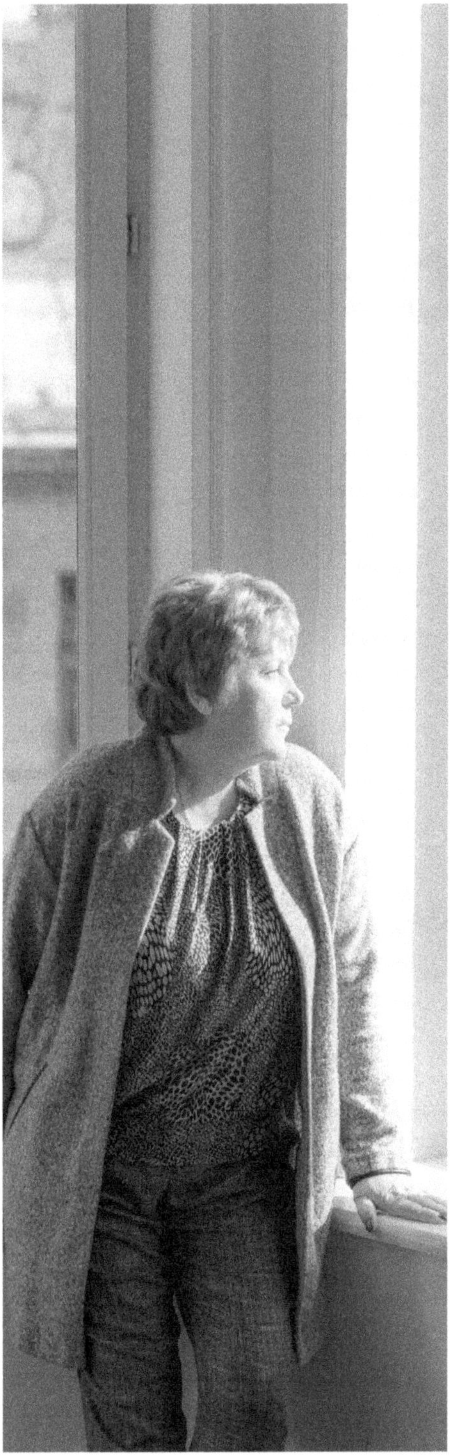

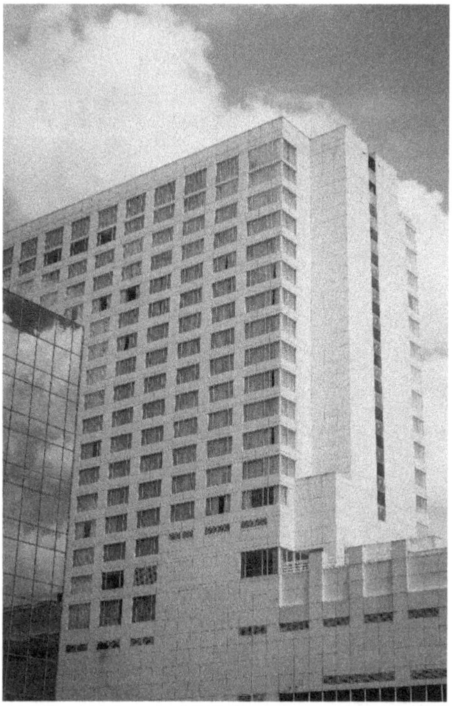

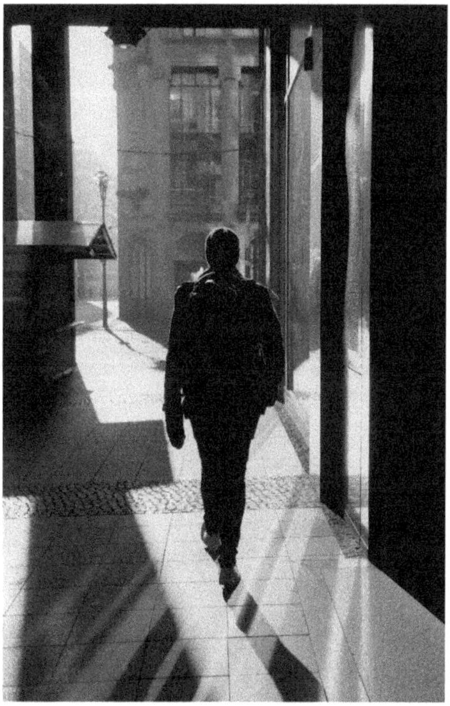

CHAPTER 7

Get Out

○ ○ ○

"There is no use for thinking outside the box and discovering a world that is out there, only to stay in the one that limits us. This may seem like a logical and simple conclusion to you, but this step can be harder than you think. There is a serious discrepancy between perceiving what needs to happen and actually making it happen by taking action."

READ / Chapter 7

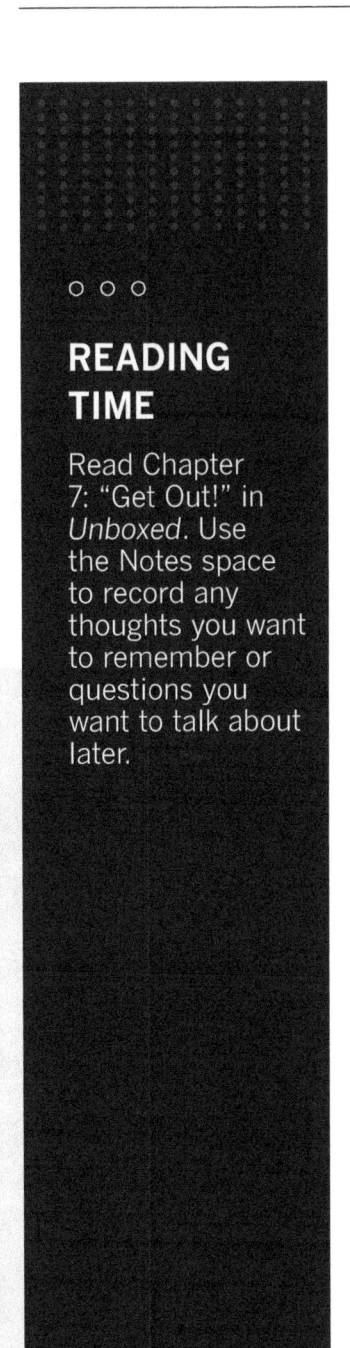

READING TIME

Read Chapter 7: "Get Out!" in *Unboxed*. Use the Notes space to record any thoughts you want to remember or questions you want to talk about later.

OPENING THOUGHTS /

As a leader, why is it so important to move from understanding the boxes that limit you to actually stepping outside of them?

_____
_____
_____
_____
_____

Why do you think so many people are satisfied with merely understanding their boxes? Can you think of any cultural values or pressures that contribute to this inaction?

_____
_____
_____
_____
_____

Unboxed: Study Guide | 49

○ ○ ○

STUDY SCRIPTURE

Read 2 Kings 2:5-7: "Now the sons of the prophets who were at Jericho came to Elisha and said to him, 'Do you know that the Lord will take away your master from over you today?' So he answered, 'Yes, I know; keep silent!' Then Elijah said to him, 'Stay here, please, for the Lord has sent me on to the Jordan.' But he said, 'As the Lord lives, and as your soul lives, I will not leave you!' So the two of them went on. And fifty men of the sons of the prophets went and stood facing them at a distance, while the two of them stood by the Jordan."

○ ○ ○

According to this passage and this chapter, what allowed the prophets to see things that others couldn't see?

_____
_____
_____
_____
_____

How do we know that these same prophets failed to reach Step 3 in the process? What didn't they do?

_____
_____
_____
_____
_____

Why do you think the prophets, who had foretold Elijah's departure, were actually surprised when it happened? What does this reveal about their hearts?

_____
_____
_____
_____
_____

50 | Get Out

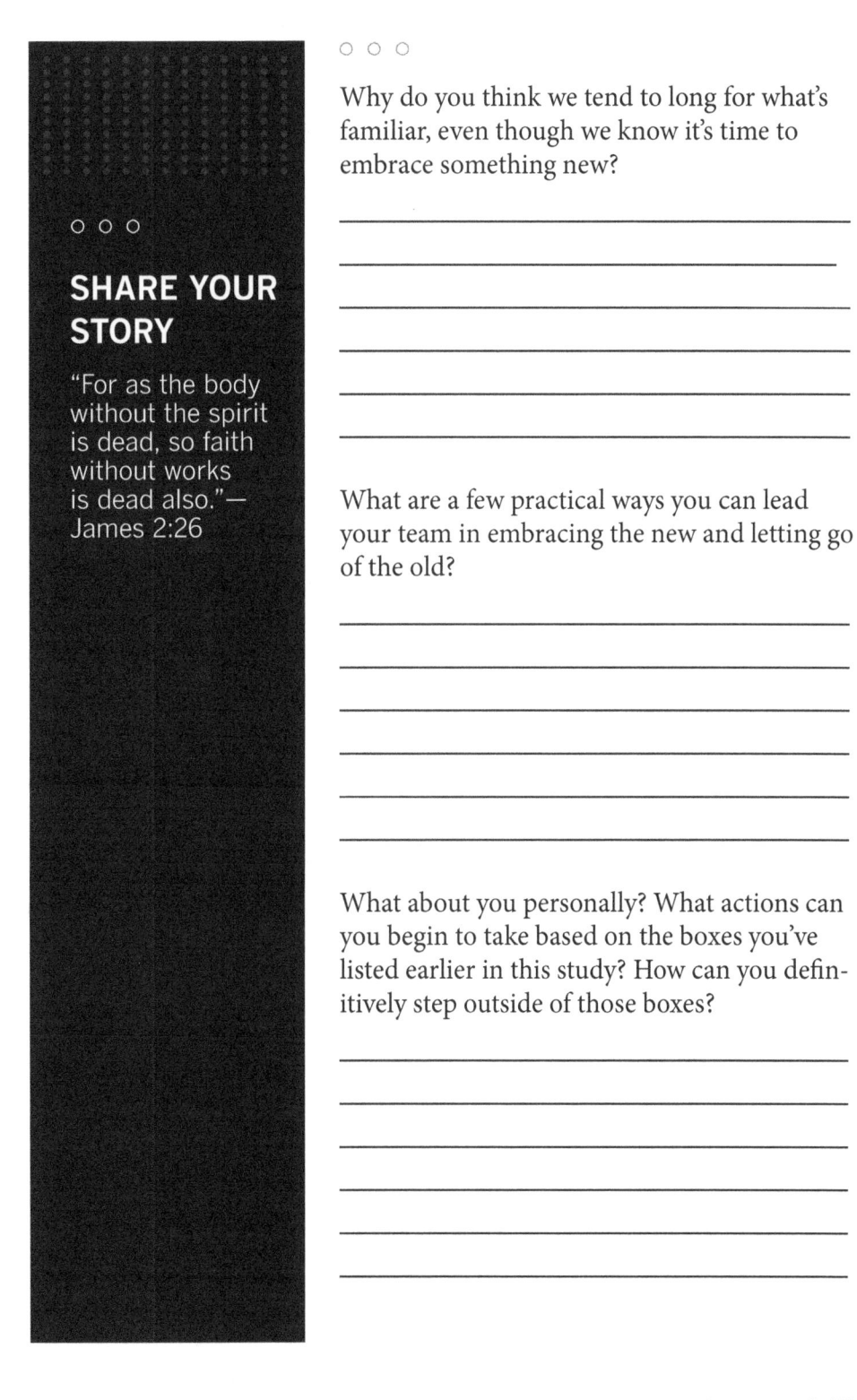

○ ○ ○

SHARE YOUR STORY

"For as the body without the spirit is dead, so faith without works is dead also."—James 2:26

○ ○ ○

Why do you think we tend to long for what's familiar, even though we know it's time to embrace something new?

_____
_____
_____
_____
_____
_____

What are a few practical ways you can lead your team in embracing the new and letting go of the old?

_____
_____
_____
_____
_____
_____

What about you personally? What actions can you begin to take based on the boxes you've listed earlier in this study? How can you definitively step outside of those boxes?

_____
_____
_____
_____
_____
_____

○ ○ ○

Can you think of anyone— either a historical figure, a modern public figure, or an acquaintance or friend— who you've seen pass up an opportunity to step outside of the box? What box kept them contained?

_____
_____
_____
_____

How does staying inside of the box hold you back from fulfilling your personal purpose? What about your team?

_____
_____
_____
_____

Elisha told the prophets to be silent— he knew they weren't trying to help him, but rather to hold him back from where he needed to be. What voices might you need to silence in your life in order to step outside of the box?

_____
_____
_____
_____

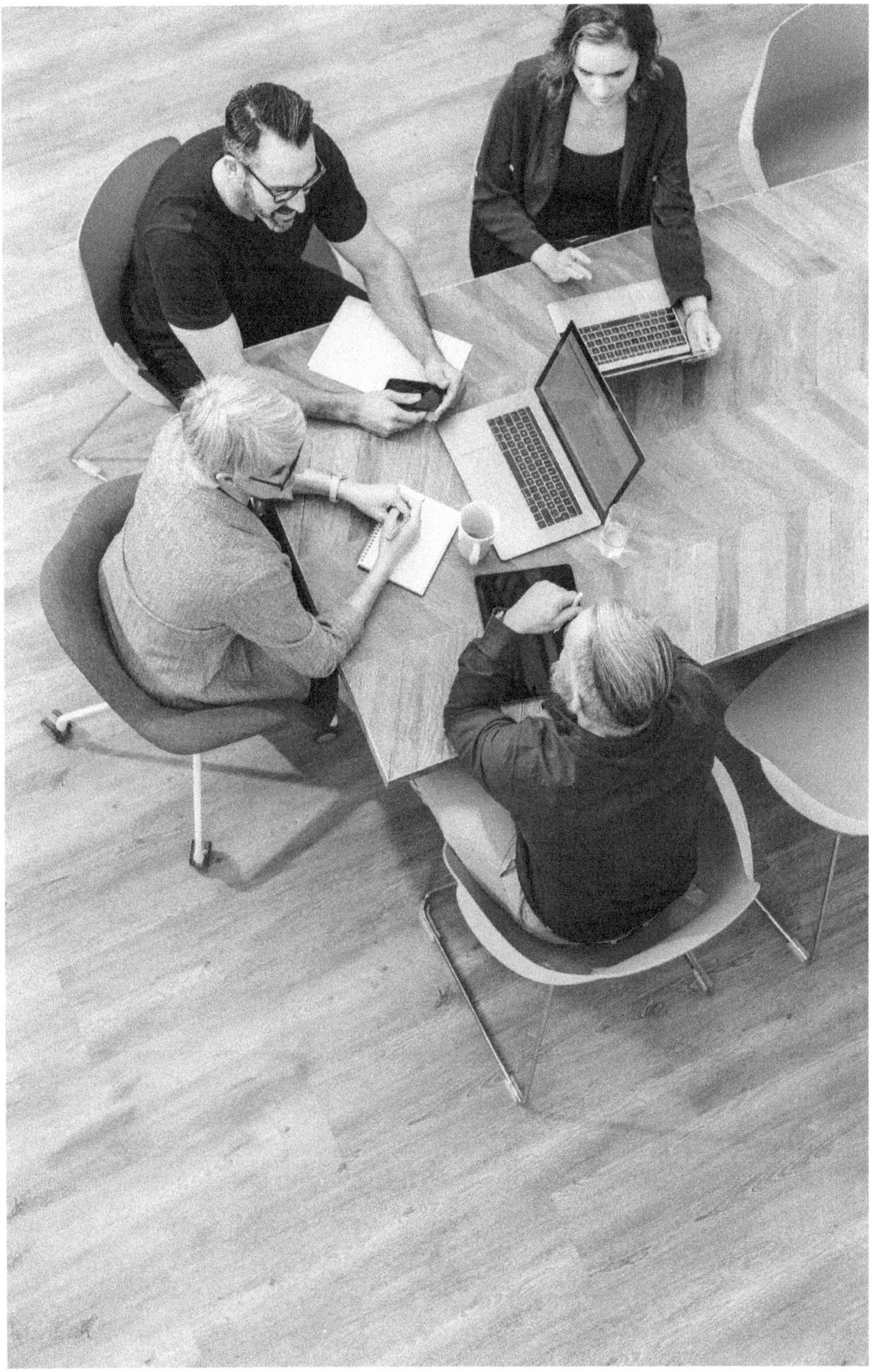

CHAPTER 8

Destroy the Box

○ ○ ○

"You are going to need to destroy your box and remove it from your reality completely—in fact, any and all boxes from your past. Somehow you are going to have to destroy those boxes that once controlled your thinking and limited the abundant life that God has destined you for."

READ / Chapter 8

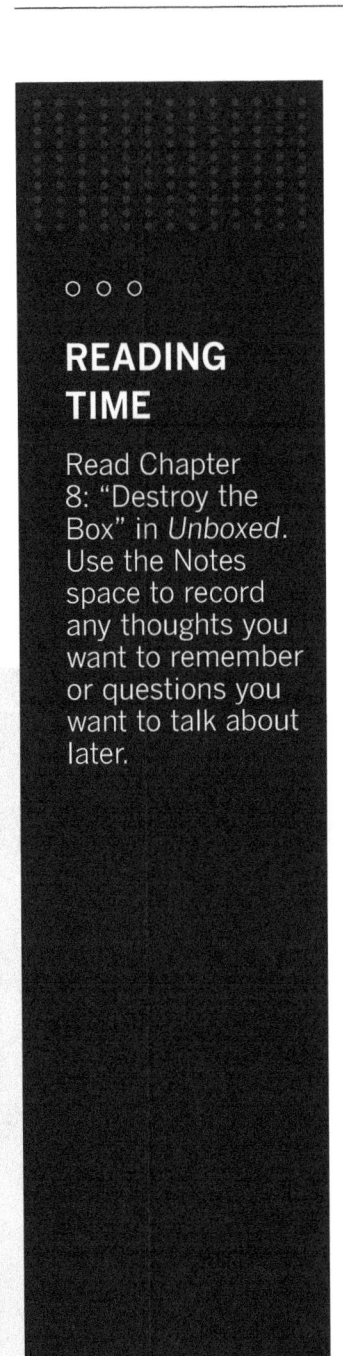

OPENING THOUGHTS /

Why do you think it's dangerous to leave a box in your life, even if you've stepped out of it?

_____
_____
_____
_____
_____
_____

Are there any boxes in your life that you've stepped out of, but that haven't been destroyed? If so, what are those thought patterns?

_____
_____
_____
_____
_____
_____
_____
_____

READING TIME

Read Chapter 8: "Destroy the Box" in *Unboxed*. Use the Notes space to record any thoughts you want to remember or questions you want to talk about later.

○ ○ ○

STUDY SCRIPTURE

Read Joshua 5:13-14: "And it came to pass, when Joshua was by Jericho, that he lifted his eyes and looked, and behold, a Man stood opposite him with His sword drawn in His hand. And Joshua went to Him and said to Him, 'Are You for us or for our adversaries?' So He said, 'No, but as Commander of the army of the Lord I have now come.' And Joshua fell on his face to the earth and worshiped."

○ ○ ○

What circumstances do you think contributed to Joshua's "either/or" mindset in this moment?

_____
_____
_____
_____
_____
_____

Can you identify any cultural or societal values that contribute to an "either/or" mindset in your life right now?

_____
_____
_____
_____
_____
_____

Why do you think boxes are difficult to destroy? Are there any boxes you've found particularly difficult to get rid of in your own life?

_____
_____
_____
_____
_____
_____

SHARE YOUR STORY

"Where Joshua (or you and me) tend to think within a limited number of possibilities, God always thinks bigger. In His mind, our little self-fabricated truths keep us from thinking bigger and beyond."

○ ○ ○

In your own words, what does Martijn mean when he says that boxes left un-destroyed result in an "anti-behavior"?

_____
_____
_____
_____
_____
_____

How will destroying our boxes improve our relationships with others— even those who believe the same paradigms we've gotten rid of in our own lives?

_____
_____
_____
_____
_____
_____

Have you ever jumped out of a box, only to return to it later on? What did this process look like for you?

_____
_____
_____
_____
_____
_____

○ ○ ○

Jeremiah was called to destroy certain things by God. What things might you be called to destroy in your personal calling? What about in your leadership?

___

Think about the story of Solomon's temple. Why do you it's easy to assume that something being destroyed means that it wasn't valuable or meaningful?

___

How could destroying certain things—even things that have been helpful and beneficial in the past—provide an even bigger benefit for you and your team moving forward?

___

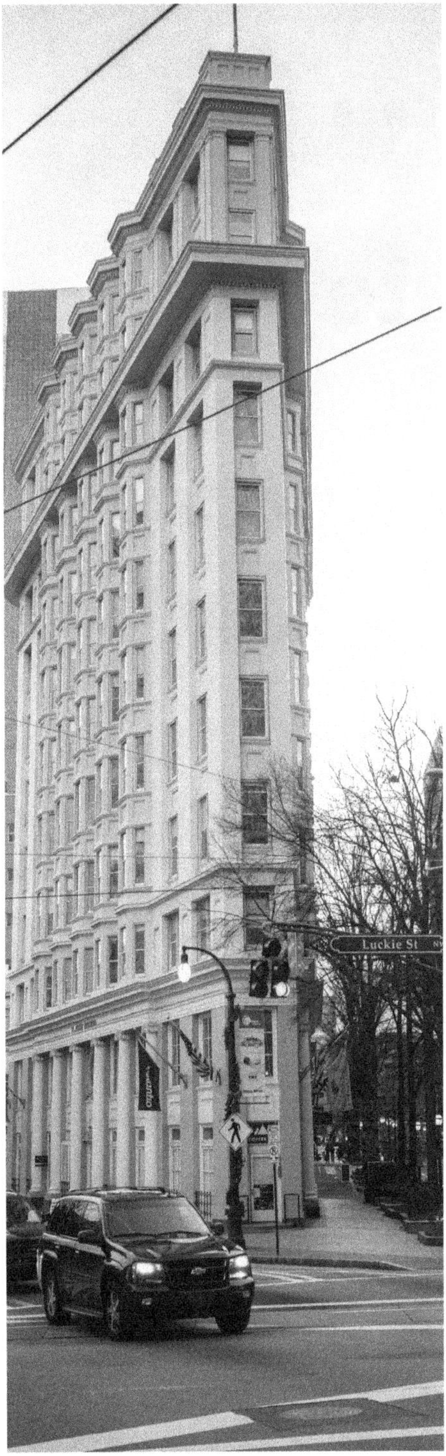
Luckie St
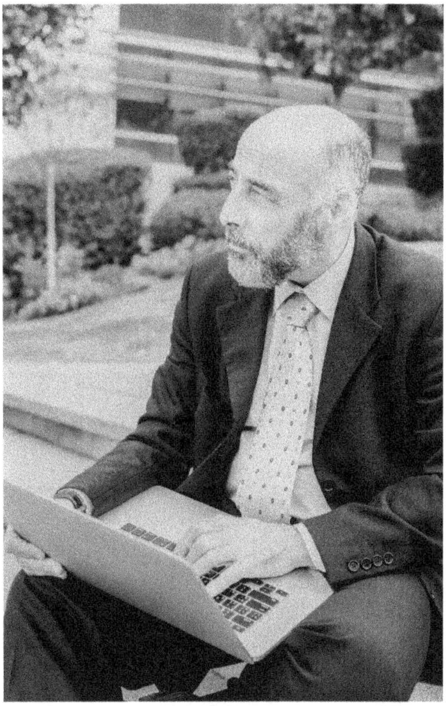
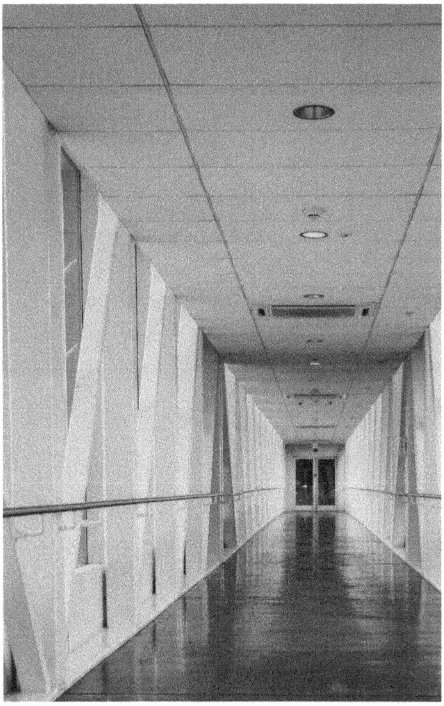

CHAPTER 9

Create

○ ○ ○

"Step 5 is all about creating something...something that can only be authentically defined by you. It can be a lonely process because only you and you alone can
take this part of the journey."

READ / Chapter 9

OPENING THOUGHTS /

Why do you think God planted in each of us the desire to create something utterly unique?

_____
_____
_____
_____
_____
_____

Can you pinpoint anything in your life and leadership journey that you've created—something original, one-of-a-kind (hint: it could even be a concept or a new way of doing things)?

_____
_____
_____
_____
_____
_____

READING TIME

Read Chapter 9: "Create" in *Unboxed*. Use the Notes space to record any thoughts you want to remember or questions you want to talk about later.

STUDY SCRIPTURE

Read Ephesians 3:8-11: "To me, who am less than the least of all the saints, this grace was given, that I should preach among the Gentiles the unsearchable riches of Christ, and to make all see what is the fellowship of the mystery, which from the beginning of the ages has been hidden in God who created all things through Jesus Christ; to the intent that now the manifold wisdom of God might be made known by the church to the principalities and powers in the heavenly places, according to the eternal purpose which He accomplished in Christ Jesus our Lord."

○ ○ ○

Paul understood that he didn't deserve to be a saint, based on his past. However, he could have allowed his past to distract him or even disqualify him from God's calling on his life. How has the enemy used your past to try to distract you from your purpose?

_____
_____
_____
_____
_____
_____

Paul knew what he was here to do— he knew he had a bright future and a purpose. Do you have a clear vision of what God's grace has appointed you to do?

_____
_____
_____
_____
_____
_____

How does it make you feel to know that God is such a creative God— that He's so creative, in fact, that we will never fully grasp the breadth of His creative expression?

_____
_____
_____
_____

SHARE YOUR STORY

"There are so many sides to God's creative expression that it would be impossible for one man to determine the parameters of what this could look like. In fact, collectively as human beings, we would not be able to define the boundaries of the potential of His creative expression, as He does more than what we can even think or imagine."

○ ○ ○

Why is it so crucial for leaders to have a creative mindset? How can a lack of creativity get leaders in trouble?

_____
_____
_____
_____
_____
_____

In your own words, explain the difference between uniformity and unity.

_____
_____
_____
_____
_____
_____

Have you seen uniformity, or lack of creativity, actually turn people, prospects, or business away from you? Why do you think this is?

_____
_____
_____
_____
_____
_____

○ ○ ○

Why is it necessary to remove the box from your life before beginning to create?

_____
_____
_____
_____

What is God calling you to create? What's that unique vision or purpose He's placed on your heart?

_____
_____
_____
_____

How about your team and organization— what dream has He given you and your people?

_____
_____
_____
_____

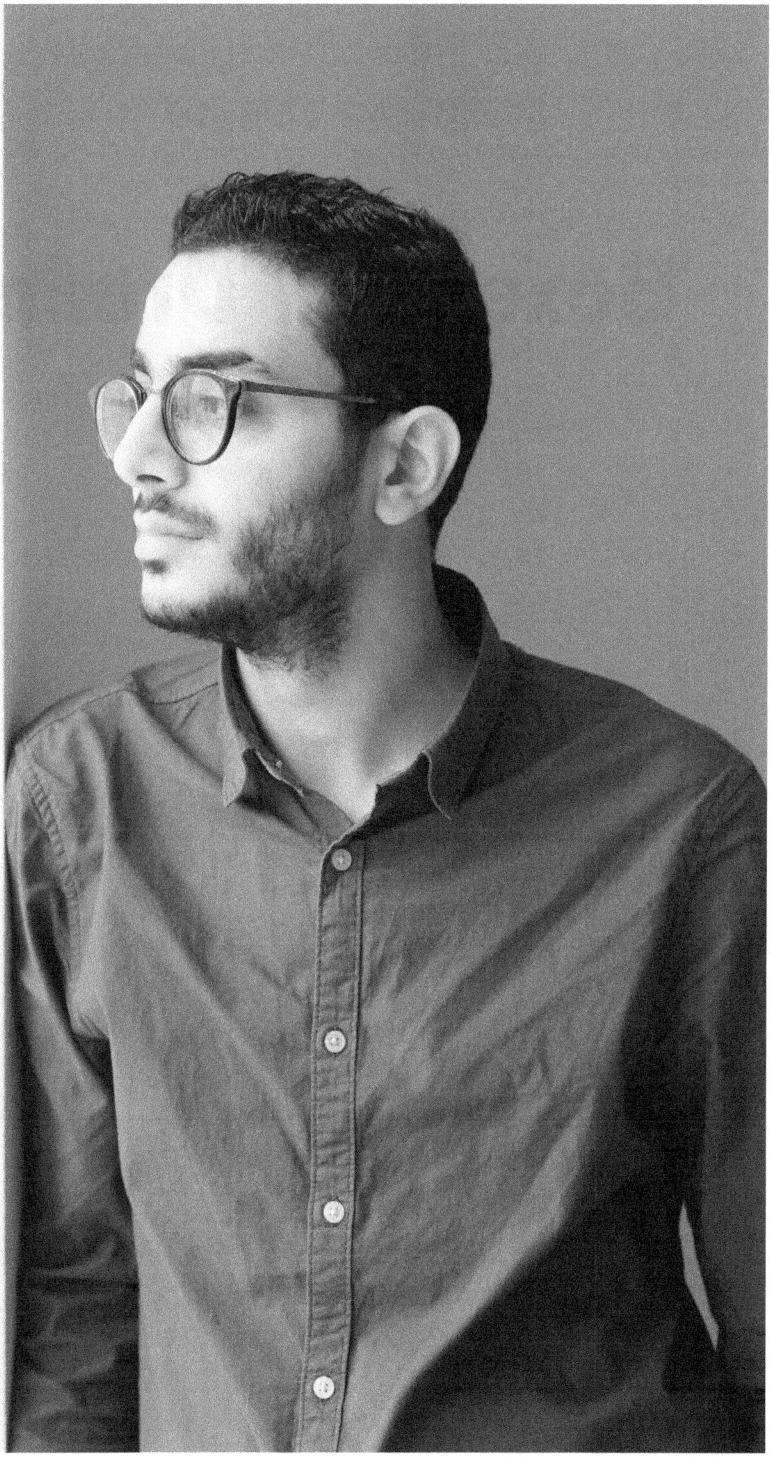

CHAPTER 10

Boxes Kill Dreams

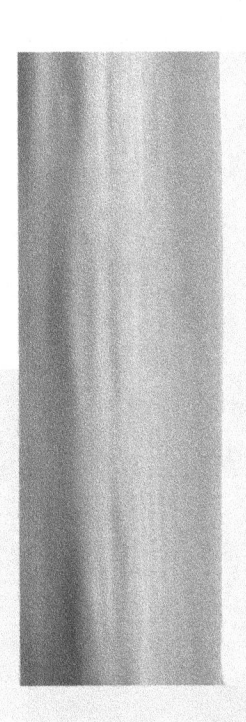

○ ○ ○

"As leaders, our primary task is to facilitate an environment in the church where this process can take place. We need to develop a culture and climate where God can simply pour out His Spirit. A place where He can show up and release dreams and visions to all flesh."

READ / Chapter 10

READING TIME

Read Chapter 10: "Boxes Kill Dreams" in *Unboxed*. Use the Notes space to record any thoughts you want to remember or questions you want to talk about later.

OPENING THOUGHTS /

What are some things leaders can do to begin to facilitate this environment for their people?

_____
_____
_____
_____
_____
_____

In your specific organization, how can you begin to foster this culture? What are 1-2 practical steps you can take?

_____
_____
_____
_____
_____
_____

○ ○ ○

STUDY SCRIPTURE

Read Joel 2:28-32: "...I will pour out My Spirit on all flesh; your sons and your daughters shall prophesy, Your old men shall dream dreams, your young men shall see visions. And also on My menservants and on My maidservants I will pour out My Spirit in those days. ... And it shall come to pass that whoever calls on the name of the Lord shall be saved."For in Mount Zion and in Jerusalem there shall be deliverance, as the Lord has said, among the remnant whom the Lord calls."

○ ○ ○

Why do you think fresh vision—a fresh dream—is more powerful than the other miracles and signs God can perform?

_____
_____
_____
_____
_____
_____

Do you currently feel like you're living in the dream God has given you? Explain your answer.

_____
_____
_____
_____
_____
_____

If those around you haven't been unboxed, they won't see your dream for what it is. Have you ever faced others' opposition to God's dream for your life? What did that look like?

_____
_____
_____
_____
_____
_____
_____

SHARE YOUR STORY

"When God gives you a dream, chances are that the people around you, especially those close to you, will not understand what it is you are seeing."

○ ○ ○

Why is it essential to make sure that we're following God's dream for our lives, and not merely our own?

_____
_____
_____
_____
_____
_____

In our competitive culture, we often feel threatened when others have a dream. How can you champion others' dreams while still pursuing your own?

_____
_____
_____
_____
_____
_____

What power is there to be found in a team that supports one another's vision, chases the overall vision of the organization, and understands that they each have an essential role to play? How could such a team change the landscape of their industry and their world?

_____
_____
_____
_____
_____

○ ○ ○

What's one big takeaway from this study that has stayed with you throughout the book? Why do you think this truth impacted you so much?

_____

_____

_____

_____

Who is someone in your life who needs your encouragement to realize, or keep pursuing, their own dream?

_____

_____

_____

_____

What's one thing you can do to help the person you listed above? How can you encourage, support, and urge them onward?

_____

_____

_____

_____

Unboxed: Study Guide | 71

CPSIA information can be obtained
at www.ICGtesting.com
Printed in the USA
FSHW020611110620